Beyond the Bog Coat

...a creative clothing workbook...

by Linda Halpin

RCW
PUBLISHING COMPANY

Cover Photo: *Left to Right:*
Juliann Kravec: Child's jungle print Bog Coat with Strip-Pieced inserts in banding
Amanda Halpin: Short Bog Coat with Peplum, elastic at waist, Seminole Patchwork banding, and sleeves pleated into a cuff

Dedication

To my Mom,
Rose Mary Fedele,
who taught me to sew and never yelled at me
when I got into her fabrics to make clothes for my dolls

Acknowledgments

A special thank you to my models
Amanda Halpin, Jamie Kravec, Jody Kravec, Juliann Kravec, Flora Newton, and Lynn Shepson;
to Jeanne Wilber, Amanda Halpin, Lynn Shepson, and Ann Marie Sanders
who generously loaned their coats for the pictures in this workbook;
and to Lynn Balassone, RCW graphic designer

Credits:

Photography by Stephen J. Appel Photography, Vestal, New York
Location: Steele Memorial Library, Elmira, New York
Mural Artwork by Pauline Emery
Stuffed Animals from the collection of Ann Brouse

Beyond the Bog Coat©
©1993 by Linda Halpin
Rebecca C. Wilber Publishing Company
RR #3, Old Post Lane
Columbia Cross Roads, Pennsylvania   16914-9535
717-549-3331

ISBN 0-9627646-5-5

Index of Techniques:

Left to Right:
Amanda Halpin: Waist Length Bog Coat with piping accents
Jamie Kravec: Child's Bog Coat with Curved Strip Piecing and piping accents
Jody Kravec: Tunic Length Bog Coat with Appliqué Overlay and piping accents

History Behind the Bog Coat

The first version of the bog coat I ever saw was in Jean Ray Laury's book *Quilted Clothing* (1982). Made by Ann DeWitt, it was a very simple garment that was not sewn at the underarm-bodice, but rather, laced, so it could be unlaced, laid flat, and used as a picnic blanket.

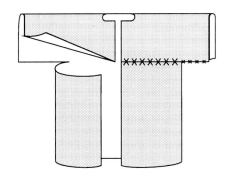

In 1984, Margot Carter Blair did an article in *Flying Needle* magazine stating that the bog coat was found in excavations in Denmark. Its basic rectangular design made it ideal for use by cultures which wove their own textiles, as there was virtually no waste of fabric in making the garment. Similar versions were therefore popular all over the world. She also commented that this basic style appeared in Egypt in 600 A.D. and was probably the influence for the Persians who made similar garments out of felt as late as the 1800's.

Virginia Avery also discusses the Bog Coat in her book *Wonderful Wearables*. She states that it was originally unearthed in Denmark about 1000 B.C. and has appeared periodically in different cultures ever since, including India, Iran, and Canada. Because of the way it is constructed out of one large piece, there is some conjecture that this type of garment may have been made out of animal skins when fabric was not yet available.

My version is a little different in that I use a front/neck band similar to those found on Japanese kimonos. This bit of detailing is very flattering to the face, and helps to make it adaptable to many body shapes. Also, my coat is reversible, the only interpretation of the Bog Coat that I know of that is. It's a wonderful pattern as is, but when you can get two garments in one by making it reversible, that's even better.

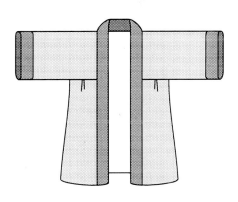

We shall explore a variety of embellishment ideas and techniques while making our own Bog Coat. Enclosed you will find photos of several versions of the Bog Coat to give you ideas for the future, and assist you in the selection of your fabrics.

Very simply patterned, the Bog Coat begins as a rectangle, the size of which is determined by how long you want the garment to be and how wide it needs to be to go around you. The rectangle is then cut and folded in such a way so as to form a coat. Made to hang open in the front, there are no closures to deal with. It is a loose-fitting jacket comparable to the weight of a sweater. Your choice of fabrics and embellishments can either dress it up or dress it down, making it wonderfully adaptable to a multitude of needs.

Making the fabric reversible before the rectangle is cut and folded simplifies the lining procedure of this garment, making it ideal for even the novice in clothing construction.

Determining yardage for the Bog Coat will vary according to the type of embellishment and/or quiltmaking technique you choose to do. General yardages to help get you started are listed on the back cover.

Patterned For Your Shape:
1/4" seams are used throughout the garment. Seam allowances are built into all of the measurements we are about to take. Before cutting, there are a few basic measurements needed to determine the size of your rectangle.

GARMENT LENGTH

11" for sleeve fold-over

from top of shoulder, over bust, to desired length

←—GARMENT WIDTH—→
hip or bust (use larger)

Body of Coat

Size of rectangle is determined by:

1. How long you want the garment to be:

> Measure from the top of your shoulder over your bust to the desired length. Add 11" to this measurement (for the sleeve fold-over).
>> This is the LENGTH of the garment.

> shoulder to hem + 11" = _____ (garment length)

Example: **Tunic Length**: *Measure from the top of the shoulder over the bust to just below the fullest part of the hips. On me, that means I can cup my fingers around the hemline of my tunic length coats. (30") To this measurement, add 11" for the sleeve fold-over, for a total 'garment length' of 41".*

NOTE: Don't get confused. While this is referred to as the **length**, it is not necessarily the longest edge of the rectangle you are about to make.

2. How wide the rectangle has to be to go around your body with ease for movement built in:

> Measure your bust and hips. Use the larger measurement. Additional ease will be built in when we add the bands.
>> This is the WIDTH of the garment.

> hip or bust (use the larger) = _____ (garment width)

NOTE: It is also referred to as the width of the rectangle, even though it may be the longer edge of the rectangle.

The actual size of the rectangle you will start with will depend on the variation of the Bog Coat you choose to make.

Bands:

Bands added to sleeves and around the front/neck edge soften the silhouette of the garment to give a more flattering line. They also serve to build in ease so the garment fits comfortably. They are cut like so:

Sleeve Bands:
> Cut 2 for the inside and 2 for the outside of the coat (a total of 4):
> *width:* 3 1/2" wide
> *length:* 22" long (to fit on the 11" fold-over that forms the sleeve)

Front / Neck Bands:
> Cut 1 for the inside and 1 for the outside of the coat (a total of 2):
> *width:* 3 1/2" wide
> *length:* (GARMENT LENGTH multiplied by 2, minus 12"*)
> *TRUST ME... IT WORKS..

> *Example:* For my Tunic Length Bog Coats, my garment length is 41".
>> 41" multiplied by 2 is 82".
>> 82" minus 12" is 70".
>> My front/neck bands are then 3 1/2" wide, 70" long

The front/neck bands are cut on the 44" width of the fabric and pieced to achieve the required length. Join strips with a straight seam at what will be the center back neck. When attaching the front/neck band to the garment, you may position the seam at the center back, where it will be least noticeable.

Optional piping on front and sleeve bands:

An easy way to add a fine line of accent is to insert piping along the sleeve and front/neck band seams. To do so:

        sleeves:

                cut 2:   *width:* 3/4"

                            length: 22"

        front/neck band:

                cut 1:   *width* 3/4"

                            length: length of front/neck band*

                            *If it is necessary to seam pieces to achieve desired length, do so on an angle to reduce bulk.

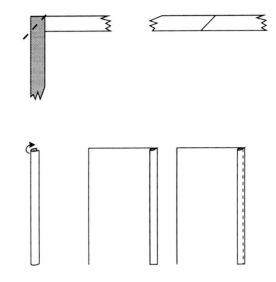

1. Press piping strips in half, wrong sides together, raw edges even, so piping is 3/8" wide.

2. Place folded strip on right side of bands, raw edges even, along one long edge. (Match center back seams of front/neck band and its piping)

3. Baste within seam allowance through all three layers. (Placing the basting within the seam allowance will eliminate the need to remove the basting once the band is sewn to the garment.)

4. When applying the bands to the garment with a standard 1/4" seam, the result is 1/8" piping.

HINT: To achieve a piping that is of uniform width:
Position basting stitches a uniform distance from the FOLD of the piping rather than from the raw edge. Use this basting as a stitching guide when attaching the band to the garment.

Now that you know how to determine the size of the pieces you need for your reversible coat, here's the general procedure you will be following. It shows how the garment takes shape. Specific step-by-step directions follow.

General Procedure:

1. Place Body of Coat fabrics for Sides One and Two wrong sides together. Quilt the two layers together, thereby making a reversible piece of cloth.

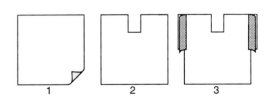

2. Remove neck section.

3. Add sleeve bands.

4. Fold along shoulder fold.

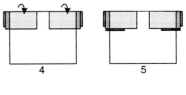

5. Cut 1/4 of the way in to form underarms.

6. Fold the resulting side flaps in.

7. Add front/neck band.

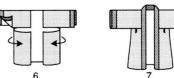

8. Bind raw edges.

Left to Right:
Jody Kravec: Tunic Length Bog Coat with Seminole Patchwork banding
Jamie Kravec: Balloon Bog Coat with Strip-Pieced bands and rolled back cuffs
Amanda Halpin: Waist Length Bog Coat with diagonal plaid banding, black piping accents, and sleeves pleated into a cuff

Cutting Requirements

Having a checklist for the ingredients you need is extremely helpful. Fill in the sizes required for each piece, as well as a fabric description. 1/4" seams are built into the measurements taken previously. **1/4" seams are used throughout the construction of the coat.**

Side One:

Body of Coat :   cut 1   size:
                                   Fabric description:

*Position the **length of the garment** on the **width of the cloth**. If your fabric is directional, see page 26 (Working with Striped Fabric or One-Way Designs) for hints on special treatment of fabric. Remember that the length of the garment is not necessarily the longer edge of the rectangle!*

Front/Neck Band: cut 1*   size:
                                   Fabric description:

Sleeve Bands: cut 2   size: 3 1/2" x 22"
                                   Fabric description:

Optional Piping: cut 1 (for front/neck band)   size:
                                   Fabric description:

                     cut 2 (for sleeves) size: 3/4" x 22"
                                   Fabric description:

The front/neck bands are cut on the 44" width of the fabric and pieced to achieve the required length. If you are using a band that has a definite pattern to it (ex: border stripe, Seminole Patchwork, etc.), match the pattern at the center back seam so the design mirrors itself as it moves away from the seam. This will result in designs matching each other at the center front.

Side Two:

Body of Coat :   cut 1**   size:
                                   Fabric description:

***Before cutting, see **Construction: Garment** (page 10) for a timesaving hint*

Front/Neck Band: cut 1   size:*
                                   Fabric description:

Sleeve Bands: cut 2   size: 3 1/2" x 22"
                                   Fabric description:

Optional Piping: cut 1 (for front/neck band) size:
                                   Fabric description:

                     cut 2 (for sleeves) size: 3/4" x 22"
                                   Fabric description:

Binding:

(Directions for determining the size square needed for binding
and how to make binding begin on page 13)

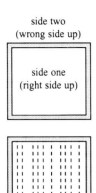

side two
(wrong side up)

side one
(right side up)

HINTS:
Be sure your bobbin is full before you begin sewing.
* *You may use one color of thread in the bobbin and a contrasting color of thread on top, if desired.*
For best stitch quality, use the same brand of thread in both positions.

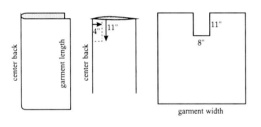

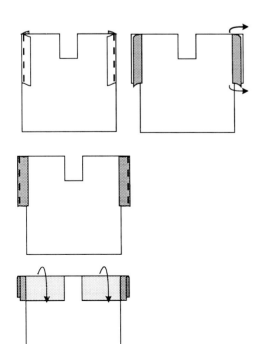

Construction

Garment:

1. Cut the 'body of the coat' for Side One.

2. Place Side One fabric WRONG SIDES TOGETHER with the fabric for Side Two. Pin at frequent intervals, making small bites with your pins to retain the most accuracy. Use the Side One piece as your 'pattern' for cutting Side Two. Trim so there is approximately 1" excess Side Two fabric surrounding Side One Fabric. This gives you a margin for error.

Placing the fabrics WRONG sides together gets you in position for step 3.

3. Stitch through both layers of the body of the coat in the pattern of your choice so the two layers are anchored together every 3" to 6". Remove all pins. Press.

Stitching in lines (straight or curved, as you choose) parallel with the banding (up and down the length of the garment ... lines of stitching on my Tunic Length Coat are 41" long, for example) will be more slenderizing. Stitching straight lines that are of varying distances apart gives a designer flair to the garment.

4. Remove the neck section as follows: Fold the quilted rectangle along the center back. At the top of the garment, measure 4" from the center (this will give you an 8" section when open). Remove a rectangle 8" wide by 11" long. *(See diagram if you are uncertain as to where this is).*

5. Sleeve bands may now be added to the sides of the rectangle as shown. Place the Side One sleeve bands right sides together with Side One of the coat, raw edges even. Pin in place. Now place the bands for Side Two of the coat right sides together with Side Two, in the same manner. This results in the coat being sandwiched between the two sleeve bands.

NOTE: If the bands have piping basted to them, the edge with the piping is the edge that aligns with the sides of the rectangle.

6. Stitch through all 4 layers, thereby attaching the sleeve bands. (There will be more layers if there is piping along the bands) Open the sleeve bands, placing them wrong sides together. This conceals the seam that attached the bands to the coat. If the bands had piping basted to them, you will now see a narrow 1/8" piping in the seamline. Press.

7. Baste raw edges of sleeve bands together for ease in handling.

8. Fold coat along shoulder fold. Make sure the fold is 11" deep along its entirety. Pin layers together to prevent them from shifting.

NOTE: Because this coat is reversible, the underarm-bodice seam you are about to create needs special treatment. One side of the coat will have a standard seam. The other side of the coat will have the seam allowance on it. It will be covered by the addition of a strip of cloth which conceals the seam allowance. Decide which side of the coat you want the concealing strip to be on. I recommend the side on which the print of the fabric will camouflage the strip the best.

When you fold the coat along the shoulder fold as described, the side of the coat you fold into view is the side which will have the concealing strip on it. (Another way to think of it is that the layers you are placing right sides together will have the standard seam)

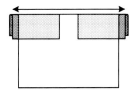

9. Measure across the fold, from end-of-sleeve band to end-of-sleeve band. *It is important to include the sleeve bands in this measurement.* Divide this measurement into fourths. _____.

10. Using the one-quarter measurement found above, measure along the bottom of the sleeve, from the END OF THE BAND toward the center, 1/4 of the way in. *Include the sleeve bands in this measurement.* Cut to this point. This will become the underarm seam. Do this under both the left and the right sleeves.

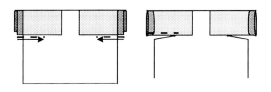

11. Stitch a 1/4" seam along the underarm of the sleeve, ending stitching 1/4" PAST the cut made in step 10 with a lockstitch. (To lockstitch, set stitch length at 0 and let the needle go up and down 4 or 5 times.)

12. The lower flaps created when you made the underarm cut will now be folded around to form the front of the coat. For ease in handling, clip the COAT (not the sleeve) from where the sleeve cut (step 10) ended to where the stitching ends (step 11) with a 1/4" diagonal clip.

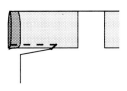

13. To join the segments marked with an 'x', gently gather or pleat the lower sections to fit the bodice sections (I prefer pleats because they are more slenderizing). Position the pleats midway in the space available.

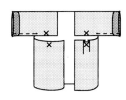

Pin, then stitch with a 1/4" seam. This gives you the underarm-bodice seam on the **outside** of the garment.

14. Measure the underarm-bodice seam. Cut two strips this length that are 2" wide. Press the strips in half, wrong sides together, raw edges even.

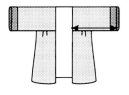

15. Position one strip along the underarm-bodice seam, laying on the BACK OF THE SLEEVE, AND THE PLEATED PORTION OF THE SKIRT, with raw edges even. Pin in place.

16. Re-stitch the underarm-bodice seam, using the original stitching as a guide to attach the folded strip.

Repeat on the remaining underarm-bodice seam. BE SURE THE STRIP IS IN THE SAME POSITION ON BOTH LEFT & RIGHT FRONT.

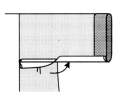

17. Press the strip and the seam up so they lay flat all the way across the sleeve. When doing so, the band conceals the seam. Appliqué or blindstitch the folded strip in place, being careful that your stitches do not go through to the other side of the coat.

Front Band:

This is added in three separate sewing steps to avoid pleats or tucks in the corners.

1. Pin the Side One front/neck band to its side of the coat, RIGHT SIDES TOGETHER, raw edges even, matching the center back seam of the front/neck band to the center back of the garment. *Match edges along the 8" edge of the neck opening only.*

2. Now pin the Side Two front/neck band to its side of the coat, RIGHT SIDES TOGETHER in the same manner. This will result in the coat being sandwiched between the two front/neck bands. There will be excess front/neck band flopping at both ends of the 8" segment of the neck opening of both Sides One and Two of the coat. This is correct.

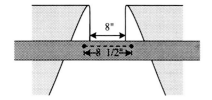

3. Stitch with a 1/4" seam, starting and stopping 1/4" beyond the cut edge of the neck opening, LOCKSTITCHING at the beginning and end of the seam. (Your line of stitching will be 8 1/2" long) Remove the garment from the machine, clip threads.

4. For ease in handling, peel back the seam allowances of the front/neck bands, exposing the reversible coat fabric, and make a diagonal clip 1/4" long from the corner of the neck opening to the lockstitching.

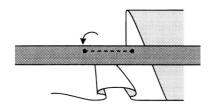

5. The clip will allow you to straighten the front of the coat in alignment with the 8" neck opening edge so you may easily pin and stitch the front/neck bands to the second edge of the neck opening in the same manner.

Stitch from where you lockstitched previously to the bottom edge of the coat, *lockstitching* at the beginning of your stitching and *backstitching* at the bottom edge of the coat.

6. Repeat with the remaining front edge of the coat. THERE WILL BE EXCESS front/neck band at the bottom edge of the coat. THIS WAS MARGIN FOR ERROR. TRIM OFF EXCESS AT THIS TIME.

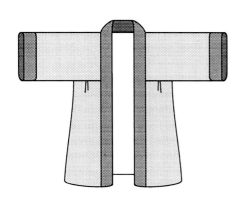

7. Press open the front/neck band so the raw edges align (as you did with the sleeve bands). The seam you just made is now encased and hidden. Baste the raw edges of the front/neck bands together for ease in handling.

8. The only things left to finish are the raw edges on the 'ends of the sleeves' and 'up the front/around the neck/down the front/around the hem' of the garment.

Cut bias binding according to the following directions 2" wide, and apply as for a quilt, starting binding along the bottom edge, near the center back, and mitering in the corners at the bottom of the coat.

Tunic Length Bog Coat with Seminole Patchwork banding with piping accents. Hand-dyed fabrics were used for the Seminole Patchwork to achieve coloration that undulates around the edging of the garment.

Continuous Bias Tape with a Rotary Cutter

To figure yardage:
To find HOW LARGE A SQUARE TO START WITH for the amount of bias you need, multiply the length (in inches) of bias you need by the width you plan to cut the bias, and find the square root. *(Most pocket calculators have a square root function button on them, so this is really easy to do.)* This will give you the size square you need to start with.

Example: For my bog coat that measures '30" from shoulder to hem', and '42" + bands' around, I would need:
30" (length) + 3" (band) + 42" (around) + 3" (band) + 30" (length) + 8" (back neck) + 44" (2 sleeves)
a. Total bias needed = 160"
b. 160" x 2" (cut 2" wide binding) = 320"
c. The square root of 320 is 17.89

Start with a square 19" - 20" square to give yourself a margin for error.

If you want to know HOW MUCH BIAS A SQUARE WILL YIELD:
Multiply the length of the square by the width, and divide the result by the width of bias you are cutting.

Example: for a 20" square:
a. 20" x 20" = 400"
b. 400" divided by 2= 200" of bias tape (plenty for my bog coat)

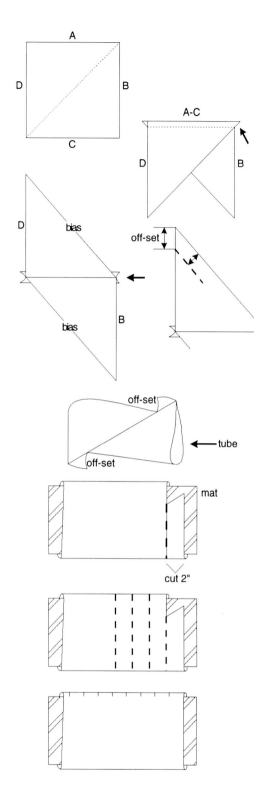

Continuous Bias Tape:

1. Cut a square of cloth. Cut in half on the diagonal. Label sides as shown.

2. Match the top (A) and bottom (C) edges of the square, right sides together, off-setting the ends 1/4" as shown, and stitch with a 1/4" seam. Press seam OPEN to reduce bulk. Lay fabric out flat.

3. Decide on the width of your bias strip. For 1/4" wide finished edging, I recommend 2". Measure 2" in from one of the BIAS edges, as shown by the dotted line. The 'straight grain edge' of the 2" strip, from the dotted line to the corner, will be the 'off-set' amount in the next step.

4. Place sides B and D right sides together, off-setting the amount achieved in Step 3.

If it looks twisted and crooked, like you did something wrong, you've done it right!

Stitch with a 1/4" seam. Press seam open. A tube has been formed. Turn tube right side out.

5. Insert a cutting mat into the tube. Position a cutting ruler (Omnigrid®, Quickline®, Salem® etc.) so the 2" mark of the ruler aligns with the bias edge of the tube, and 2" of ruler covers the fabric. Cut along this edge with a rotary cutter.

NOTE: YOU MAY ONLY CUT THROUGH ONE LAYER AT A TIME FOR THIS TO WORK!!!

6. Reposition the ruler so the 2" marking aligns with the cut just made, and 2" of ruler covers a new section of the tube. Cut. Repeat until the entire exposed surface has been cut every 2".

7. Reposition the tube on the cutting mat so an uncut expanse is exposed, leaving about 1" of slashes showing. Repeat above cutting procedure, connecting 'old cuts' with 'new cuts'.

8. Depending on the size of your tube and your mat, you may need to reposition your tube three or four times to connect the slashes. The entire tube has now been cut and can be wound off the cutting mat. To use this bias strip, press in half, wrong sides together, so the folded strip is now 1" wide. To store the folded continuous bias binding and keep it from wrinkling until you are ready to use it, wrap it around a cardboard tube.

Edge Finishing:

Professional edge finishing can be achieved by mitering the binding of your Bog Coat as you turn the corners.

1. For a 1/4" bound edge, cut continuous bias tape 2" wide. Fold in half, wrong sides together, edges even. Press. Folded bias is now 1" wide.

2. Pin folded bias to the edge you are binding, all raw edges even, starting about 4" from a corner. Begin stitching about 2" from the beginning of the bias, using a 1/4" seam, stitching through all layers.

3. To miter corners, stop stitching 1/4" from the end of the garment. Lockstitch at this point.

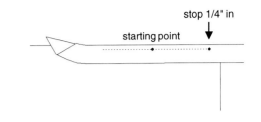

starting point

stop 1/4" in

A lockstitch is obtained when you either set the stitch length on your machine at 0, so the needle goes up and down, but the fabric doesn't move (thereby knotting it), or by dropping the feed-dogs (the ziggy zaggy things that make the fabric move). This guarantees that the line of stitching starts and stops exactly where you want it to. The danger with backstitching at this point is that the length of the stitch going forward is not always the same length as that of the stitch going backward, causing you to have a stitch where you don't want it, resulting in a pucker or pleat.

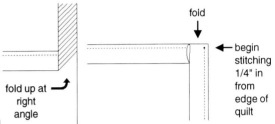

fold

fold up at right angle

begin stitching 1/4" in from edge of quilt

    a. Fold the binding up at right angles

    b. then fold binding down with the corner square. This forms a triangular pleat.

4. Begin stitching at the same point where you ended your previous stitching with a lockstitch, and continue stitching to the next corner, and repeat mitering procedure.

5. Ending binding: Stop stitching about 4" from the starting point. Remove the garment from the machine. On the unstitched portion of the 'beginning', turn under 1/2".

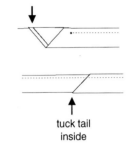

tuck tail inside

6. Cut the tail of the binding so it extends 1/2" past the fold made in step 5. Tuck the excess tail inside the folded 'beginning'. Stitch the remaining binding in place.

7. Fold the binding over the seam, encasing it. The fold of the bias will just cover the machine stitching that holds the binding to the garment. Blindstitch in place.

8. In the corners, fold binding over one edge of the garment first. This miters the binding on the front of the coat.

9. Now fold the binding to encase the second edge. This miters the binding on the back of the coat. Blindstitch the miter folds on the front and the back of the coat.

HINT:
I start/stop the binding on the coat along the bottom hem, in the back, where it will be least noticeable. On the sleeves, I start/stop on the back of the sleeve, but not at the underarm seam (there is already a lot of bulk there).

Now that you've seen how the Basic Bog Coat is constructed, explore some of the many variations...

Left to Right:
Flora Newton: Tunic Length Bog Coat with Strip-Piecing inserts
Lynn Shepson: Tunic Length Bog Coat with Border Print Banding
Jody Kravec: Tunic Length Bog Coat with Seminole Patchwork Banding and Piping accents
Juliann Kravec: Child's Bog Coat with Strip-Piecing inserts

Left to Right:
Amanda Halpin: Tunic Length Bog Coat with Seminole Patchwork banding
Jamie Kravec: Child's Bog Coat with Strip-Piecing and border print banding
Jody Kravec: Tunic Length Bog Coat with Appliqué Overlays

Variations to Length Measurement

Waist Length Bog Coat, Gathered at Hem:
Cutting:
Measure from shoulder, over bust, to 2" below waist. To this, add 11" for the sleeve fold-over.

Construction:
1. When quilting the two layers of the coat together, stop stitching 1" from bottom.

Before applying front/neck band:
2. Hem lower edge of the garment by folding raw edge of each layer under 1/4", so both seam allowances are sandwiched between the two layers of the garment. Topstitch 1/8" from folded hem edge. Make a second line of stitching 3/4" from the first. This forms a casing.

3. Insert 1/2" elastic, cutting elastic to a length that provides you with the desired fullness. Baste ends of elastic in place within seam allowance at center front edges.

4. Front/neck band may now be applied. Binding is then applied around front/neck edge.

Short Bog Coat with Peplum
(short 'skirt' below the waist):
Cutting:
Measure from shoulder, over bust, to 4" - 5" below waist. To this, add 11" for the sleeve fold-over.
> **With Elastic at Waist:** **Attach casing to one side of the coat:**
1. Cut a strip of cloth 1 1/2" wide and as long as the measurement of garment at lower edge, from band seam to band seam. Press under 1/4" on all edges.

2. Pin strip to outside of coat, 1" below natural waistline (2" - 3" up from lower edge). Stitch near the folded edge along the **long** edges of the strip. This forms a casing. Insert 1/2" elastic to a length that provides you with the desired fullness. Stitch ends of elastic in place just shy of the short ends of the casing.

3. Bind all raw edges of the garment as usual.

> **With Pleats at Waist:** You may wish to eliminate the pleats in the front of the garment for a sleeker look. To do so, simply do not form pleats when creating the underarm-bodice seam. Trim off the excess fabric that results at the center front of the garment. Add the front/neck bands as usual.

1. How many pleats you take at the back waistline and how deep they are will depend on how much fullness you wish to pull in. I used four pleats, approximately 3" apart, centered around the center back of the garment. The pleat stitching is 1 1/2" long, starting at the waist, and stitched toward the hem (ending 2 1/2" - 3 1/2" from the lower edge.)

2. The pleats (or perhaps more accurately, the tucks) may be left floating, that is, not stitched flat against the coat, if you wish.

HINT:
The band that forms the casing will be applied to the outside of the coat. If you cut a strip that has the same printed pattern motifs as the area it is covering, it will blend in with the coat and not be visible.

For Children:

Cutting:
Measure length same as for basic garment for adult. Add 3" - 6" for room to grow plus sleeve fold-over (see below). For width, add 4" - 6" to the larger of the hip or chest measurement to add room to grow. Reduce band widths from 3 1/2" to 2 1/2".

Construction:

For toddler to age 4:	Cut neck opening 6" x 10"
	Use 10" sleeve fold-over
	Use 20" for sleeve band length
For ages 5 - 10:	Cut neck opening 7" x 11"
	Sleeve fold-over and sleeve band length is as for
	the basic garment for adults
For ages 11 and older:	Construct as for the basic garment for adults

Variations in Width Measurement

Increasing the width of the rectangle is one way to create longer sleeves. *(See Method One)* Additional methods are also discussed.

Longer Sleeves:
Method One:
Cutting:
When measuring bust and hips for the width of the garment, also measure arms, extended, from wrist to wrist. (Ease is built in when sleeve bands are added on) Use the longest measurement. If your arms are the longest measurement, this will result in a garment that is fuller through the body.

Construction:
To avoid extra fullness through the body:
1. Using the larger of the hip/bust measurements, do the following:

$$(\text{hip/bust} + 6") \text{ divided by } 4 = \underline{\hspace{1cm}}$$

When ready to make the underarm cut, fold the garment in half down the center back. Mark off this measurement *from the center back toward the cuff edge.* The resulting mark is where to stop cutting when making the underarm-bodice cut.

Method Two:
To create a design feature, add the sleeve band in the regular fashion, in a contrasting fabric, then add a second band, in the fabric of the main body of the garment, in whatever width you need to achieve the desired sleeve length. Do this *before* adding the strip that conceals the underarm/bodice seam.

Method Three:
Rather than adding sleeve bands that are cut 3 1/2" wide, add sleeve bands that are wide enough to give you the desired extra length. See method one to avoid extra fullness through body. The end of the sleeve band can be bound with binding.

Method Four:
Gather or pleat the end of the sleeve band into ribbing or a cuff.
*(See **Cuff Treatment**, page 20)*

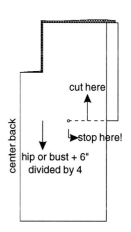

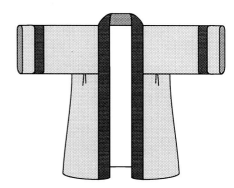

Cuff Treatment:

Elastic:

1. After making the underarm-bodice cut, but before stitching it, hem the sleeve bands by folding the long raw edge of each layer under 1/4", so both seam allowances are sandwiched between the two layers. Topstitch 1/8" from folded hem edge. Make a second line of stitching 3/4" from the first. This forms a casing.

2. Insert 1/2" elastic, cutting elastic to a length that allows you to achieve the desired fullness. Pin ends of elastic in place. They will be caught in the stitching you do next as you now stitch the underarm/bodice seam.

Pleated:

The ends of the sleeves may be pleated to absorb fullness.
    a. You could form pleats around the sleeve bands, *or*
    b. you may start at the center of the sleeve opening with a box pleat and form a series of box pleats around the edge

Once pleats are pinned in place, baste in place to eliminate pins, then apply binding to encase raw edge.

Knit Cuffs:
    a. Knit ribbing may be added to both lengthen and gather sleeves, *or*
    b. Pleat the ends of the sleeves before applying ribbing for a more tailored look.

Fabric Cuffs:

Ends of sleeve may be gathered or pleated to absorb fullness, then stitched to a fabric cuff. If this is done after the underarm/bodice cut is made, but before it is stitched, you can stitch the cuff to the sleeve while it is flat (before it becomes a ring). To achieve a lined cuff, apply in the same manner as the sleeve band. The underarm seam of the cuff can be stitched with the rest of the underarm seam, and the raw edges of the cuff bound with bias binding.

Tabbed Cuffs:

Add a tab and button to each sleeve to pull in fullness.

Batting:

Cutting:

Add 4" - 6" TO THE WIDTH AND LENGTH of your rectangle. Some of this will shrink up due to the batting. Some of this is to add the extra ease required in an outerwear garment.

Construction:

Lay batting between the Side One and Side Two fabrics when pinning them together in preparation for quilting.

Increase seams to 1/2". The seams will be bulkier due to the batting and easier to control if they are larger than the standard 1/4". Increase your sleeve foldover to 13", the neck opening to 8" x 13", and the sleeve bands to 26" long.

Strips of batting may be laid between the sleeve bands and the front/neck bands. Cut strips of batting 3" wide and the same length as the bands. After the bands have been sewn to the garment and pressed open (placing them wrong sides together), position the batting between the two layers. Quilt in place.

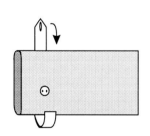

Adding batting to this garment makes it comparable to an outerwear garment rather than a sweater-weight garment. If using flannel as an inner layer for a lightweight garment, prewash several times so as to shrink the flannel before using it. If using batting, choose a batting that does not beard.

Left to Right:
Lynn Shepson: Tunic Length Bog Coat with border print banding
Amanda Halpin: Tunic Length Bog Coat with Seminole Patchwork banding
Jody Kracec: Waist Length Bog Coat with Curved Strip Piecing and Appliqué Overlays

Pockets:

Patch pockets may always be added on top of the finished coat, or you may like to insert pockets between the layers like so:

Hidden pockets are constructed before the two rectangles are quilted together. The basic rectangle is pieced in order to create in-seam pockets.
Measurements for Body of the Coat:
      garment width: hip or bust (use the larger) plus 1"
      garment length: from top of shoulder over the bust to location of desired hem plus 11"

1. Fold body of coat piece in half down the center back. Measure 8 1/4" from the raw edge where shown. Cut along this measurement, resulting in three pieces.

2. Cut 4 pockets. (Pattern is shown on page 30)

Construction:

1. Measure from hem of coat to where you want the bottom of your pocket opening. Transfer this measurement to the three coat pieces as shown to give you pocket placement guides.

2. Place pockets right sides together, raw edges even with the coat pieces, placing the bottom of the pockets even with the placement guides. Stitch with 1/4" seams. Press pockets open.

3. Place the 8 1/4" wide strips right sides together with the large coat piece, aligning pockets.

4. Stitch up seam, around pocket, and up remainder of seam. Press unit so pockets lay on the 8" wide pieces. Pin pockets in place so they don't move.

5. This newly constructed rectangle complete with pockets may now be laid with the rectangle for Side Two of the coat. When quilting the two layers together, DO NOT QUILT THROUGH THE POCKET AREA.

NOTE: If you want pockets on both Side One and Side Two of the coat, cut as above for both sides of the coat. Do steps 2 and 3 as above. THEN lay the units so the large pieces are wrong sides together, and all pockets align. (This means there will be an 8" piece on the very bottom and an 8" piece on the very top, with the two layers of the coat sandwiched between them.)

NOW do step 4, through all layers. Press open 8" pieces. You are now in position to pin and quilt the layers together. Again, DO NOT quilt through pocket areas.

Simple Seminole:

Seminole Patchwork is the perfect embellishment for Bog Coat Bands. Out of 44" - 45" wide fabric, cut strips as shown. Sew together with 1/4" seam to form a striped band. Press seams when band is complete.

Cut band into slices. Join slices as shown.

One band will yield enough slices for a Seminole band 1 1/4" wide x 33" long.

8 1/4"

1 1/2"

1 1/4"

1 1/2"

pressed band

1 1/4"

1. To determine how many Seminole bands you will need to make, add the 44" required for the two sleeve bands (22" for each sleeve) to the length required for the front/neck band. Join all slices to make one very long band.

Example: For my Tunic Length Bog Coat with a 70" long front/neck band, I need 44" (for two sleeves) + 70" (front/neck band) = 114". One sliced band will give me enough slices for 33" of Seminole Patchwork. I will need to make three and one half striped bands to result in enough slices to make 114" of Seminole Patchwork. To do so, I will need to cut four strips of each of the three fabrics shown on page 22, with each strip 44" - 45" long. Since I only need 3 1/2 of each, cutting 4 gives me a margin for error.

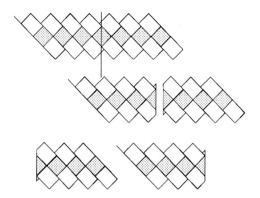

2. For the most efficient usage of the resulting Seminole band, slice the band at right angles as shown, slicing through the center of one of the Seminole motifs. This splits the band into two pieces, each with one straight end and one diagonal end.

3. Now join the diagonal ends of the resulting two pieces the same way you joined slices. This creates one long band that is squared off on the ends with no waste.

4. When you cut off the required band pieces, take care not to stretch the Seminole band. After cutting the first sleeve band, make the second sleeve band the same number of motifs long.

5. Trim off excess zig-zag edges, trimming 1/4" away from the finished corners of the squares closest to the edges of the band. This gives you straight edges instead of zig-zag edges.

Additional bands of color may now be added to the Seminole band to make it the required 3 1/2" wide.

Appliqué Overlays:
1. For a diagonal overlay, start with two pieces of cloth cut the size of the basic rectangle. Place one piece right side up. Top with the second piece, also right side up. Keeping in mind the general angle desired, cut through the *top layer only*, 1/4" larger than the printed motifs, for the desired effect.

In doing appliqué overlays on the Bog Coat, it is most helpful to make a paper mock up that you can sketch on to get an idea where everything will end up once the coat is cut and folded.

2. Pin the resulting layers in place. Clip where needed along the trimmed edge. Turn under the 1/4" seam allowance. Appliqué the top layer in place. When the appliqué is complete, you may then trim away the excess bottom layer so as to reduce bulk.

This may now be used as one new piece of cloth, and construction may begin.

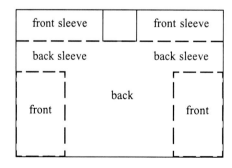

Appliqué Special Effects:
One special effect you may like to try is to allow the appliqué layer to extend past the edge of the basic layer in the area that will be along the band seams. When adding bands, fold this excess out of the way so it does not get caught in the seam. You are then free to cut around the desired motifs and do an overlay over the band that is continuous with the fabric on the coat.

Additional elegance is created when motifs are cut from printed fabric and cascaded over the surface of the coat and appliquéd in place.

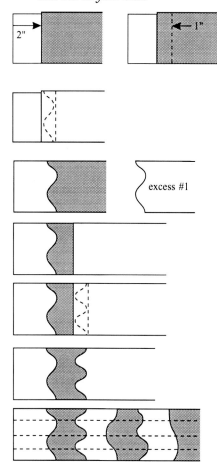

Curved Strip Piecing is a jazzy way to construct the fabric you will use in your coat.

Because everything is curvy, the cut edges are all on the bias. The stretchiness will work for you, allowing you to ease where necessary to align the edges.

Curved Strip Piecing:

For ease in handling, cut lengths of fabric 2" longer than the segment of curved strip piecing you wish to create. This gives you a margin for error.

1. Layer fabrics 1 and 2 one on top of the other, *wrong side up*, staggering the layers, so the top layer (#2) is shifted to the right exposing about 2" of the bottom layer (#1).

2. Make a guideline on fabric #2 (top layer) 1" from its cut edge.

3. Cutting smoothly (no jagged edges), cut through both fabrics, undulating your cutting line between the guideline and the cut edge of fabric #2. Gentle curves work well. Sharp curves are more difficult to join successfully.

4. Remove the scrap of fabric #2. Remove the excess of #1 from under #2. Abut #1 to #2.

5. Layer fabric #3 on top of #2, *wrong side up*, anywhere from 1" - 3" from the edge of fabric #2.

6. Mark a guideline on fabric #3, 1" from its cut edge. Cut a curving line through fabrics #2-#3 as before.

7. Remove the scrap of fabric #3. Remove the excess of #2 from under #3. Abut #2 to #3.

8. Continue until all strips have been cut and laid in position with edges abutting.

9. Draw lines through the curves of all of the fabrics approximately every 2". This will give you placement points to match when you place the strips right sides together.

10. Place #1 and #2 right sides together, pinning to match placement points. No, you didn't do anything wrong ... it's supposed to look goofy. Right now, the edges don't match (because they are curves, the convexes stick up, and the concaves scoop down, but they will match, trust me!

11. Pin so edges match, making small bites with your pins, 1/4" from the raw edge.

12. Stitch slowly with a 1/4" seam. Try to feel the underneath layer as it approaches the needle, and make sure the fabric doesn't 'pleat' on you. Remove pins as you get to them ... don't sew over them.

13. When the seam is complete, check for tucks or pleats. Repair any that may have occurred.

14. Abut the #3 strip to the 1-2 unit, matching placement points as before, and stitch.

15. When all of the strips have been added, press so seams all go in the same direction.

16. Trim piece to desired size, removing the margin for error.

Straight Strip Piecing

Straight Strip Piecing creates a more interesting texture if the strips are cut in a variety of widths. I find that cutting a range of 1", 1 1/4", 1 1/2", and 1 3/4" works well. *These measurements INCLUDE the 1/4" seam allowances.*

Hints to Remember:

 * *If you are covering the entire garment with strip piecing, begin at the center and work toward the outer edges. As you work toward the under-arm, graduate into darker values... it's more slenderizing.*

 * *If you are hippy, place a focal point in the upper yoke areas, leaving the lower areas free of eye-catching details.*

 * *It helps to have at least two 'bridge' fabrics... that is, printed fabrics whose colors link the colors of other fabrics together. This allows for a smoother transition from one color to another.*

 * *Vary the widths of the strips as you position them. Don't use too many narrow strips or it will take forever to finish the garment!*

 * *Know that the two fronts don't have to be mirror images of each other. Some of the most interesting garments have the same colors in a sequence, but use different fabrics or different widths to give it some variety.*

 * *Press seam allowances to one side. Allow the fabric to cool down before adding each new strip. Heat and steam can cause the raw edges of the fabric to stretch, making the addition of new strips more difficult and resulting in a stripped unit that does not lay flat.*

Straight Strip Piecing is a quick and easy way to create a patchwork garment.

DO NOT cut all of your fabric into strips right away. Cut one or two strips (vary the width) from each fabric so you can play with the arrangement. This gives you large pieces if you want them for other things, such as yokes, bands, pockets, etc.

When constructing the fabric used in your coat (as in Curved Strip Piecing, Straight Strip Piecing, etc.) additional embellishments may be added in the seamlines of the newly constructed fabric, such as piping, lace, and prairie points, to name a few.

Left to Right:
Lynn Shepson: Tunic Length Bog Coat with diagonal patchwork, inset pockets, and piping accents

Juliann Kravec: Child's Bog Coat with Curved Strip Piecing, zippered front, and sleeves gathered into knit ribbing

Flora Newton: Tunic Length Bog Coat with Seminole Patchwork banding

Working with Striped Fabric or One-Way Designs

First of all, for the most flattering look, you will want your stripes to go vertically on the garment (with the length of the garment), rather than around you. This will be much more slenderizing. This may mean, depending on the width of the fabric and the size rectangle you are working with, that the fabric is not wide enough. You may then have to piece it.

Adding a segment down the back generally works well. Adding to the edge of the rectangle may present design problems when you cut under the sleeve and wrap around to the front. The seam would then be on one sleeve, and near the center front on the skirt portion of one side.

If you can 'match the stripe' so the seam is not noticeable, go ahead and add an extension to the edge of the rectangle. Otherwise, consider adding it down the center back. I have done this by cutting my 'extender' so the stripes are horizontal, creating a pattern variation on the coat and giving it an 'on purpose' design rather than an 'oops, she goofed' look. You may want to use a contrasting fabric here, a Seminole Patchwork Band, or put piping along the edges of the 'extender'.

If your stripe is directional, depending on the actual design itself, you may want to make some alterations in that when you fold the fabric along the shoulder fold, the piece coming over the shoulder to the front will appear to be upside down from the rest of the garment. (This will be true with any directional fabric, not just stripes).

If you don't want the front bodice to appear upside down, make your original rectangle out of this fabric 1/2" LONGER than needed.

Cut off the top 11 1/4", flip this segment 180 degrees, and stitch it back on to the rest of the rectangle with a 1/4" seam. This means the 11" fold-over will occur at this seamline, and the direction of the bodice will be the same as on the 'skirt' of the garment. Once the 11 1/4" segment has been re-attached, you can proceed to quilt it to Side Two of the garment.

If your fabric is an even stripe, you will want to choose a particular stripe to lay down the center back. By doing so, you will have the patterning of the stripes mirroring themselves as they move away from the center back, resulting in the same motif at the center front (or edges of the original rectangle). Be aware that due to the pleating in the front, the stripes of the 'skirt' will not match the stripes of the 'bodice'. The wider the stripe, the more this discrepancy will show. Sometimes, if the stripe is very narrow, you can fudge the pleats, and they will appear to match. There is no specific guideline, however, on how to make this happen, as we are dealing with so many variables (size of original rectangle vs. size and repeat of stripes).

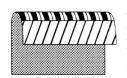

One way to camouflage the mis-match of stripes is to piece your original rectangle before it is quilted with a contrasting coordinating fabric along the top of the rectangle (this will serve as a 'buffer' between the stripes of the bodice and the stripes of the skirt when the fabric is folded along the shoulder fold). Another option would be to use a horizontal stripe here, or even one cut on the bias. (These options would require more fabric, similarly to the notation you will find on commercial patterns when stripes or fabrics with a nap are involved).

The 'buffer' could be a band of Seminole Patchwork that utilizes colors in the stripe, a segment of curved strip piecing, a section of pleated fabric, an area in which prairie points could be incorporated, etc. For continuity throughout the garment, you could use the same treatment for the neck/front banding and the sleeve banding.

Another option that works very nicely is to piece the original rectangle so the top 15"-18" is an area of contrast, with the remainder of the rectangle in vertical stripes.

> *Great techniques for areas of contrast:*
> *Curved Strip Piecing*
> *Straight Strip Piecing*
> *Patchwork*
> *Crazy Quilt Embroidery*
> *Seminole Patchwork*

By constructing the rectangle in this manner, the bodice of the coat front has special treatment when the sleeve segment is folded over, drawing the eye up to the face (and away from the hips, making it more flattering).

By doing a contrasting technique on the top 15"-18", the contrast goes on the bodice, over the shoulder and partly down the back, giving the appearance of a yoke on the back, which is very pretty. I found that if I did this segment 22" or longer from the top, there were problems when I did the under-the-sleeve cut in preparation for wrapping the sides around to the front.

Generally speaking, narrow stripes (largest being 1/2" wide) for the garment work with very little problem. Larger stripes are more successful for the accents such as bands, or pieced into the body of the garment, as opposed to using them for the overall garment.

Patchwork Special Effects:
Explore making one side of your coat either partially or entirely of patchwork. It may be the perfect way to utilize a quilt top you started but never finished. Quilting your patchwork layer to an unpieced Side Two will lend it stability as well as give you a reverse side that is totally different.

Ideas for Clothing Embellishment
Lace: newly purchased yardage or appliqués (can be tea-dyed if desired); motifs cut from lace fabric (check bridal supplies); antique: rescued from pillowcases, dresser scarves, clothing, slips, doilies, tatting (yardage or motifs)...

Appliqués: Use motifs cut from fabric: can combine elements to make larger blossoms, stitch and stuff motifs for three-dimensional embellishment, gathered or pleated motifs from fabric, can cut designs from scraps of Ultra-suede (don't have to turn under edges!)...

Ribbon: can tack down flat, outline an element on the garment, coil it, braid it, twist it, tie knots periodically, string beads on it, tie it in bows, ruche it, weave it...

Embroidery Floss: stitch added embellishments on garment...

Closures: In quilted clothing, closures are often optional. Unusual closure ideas might be:
*Ribbons that tie
*Buttons with loops rather than buttonholes
*Buttons that ribbons tie around
*Frogs (can be self-made, purchased, or rescued off of old garments)
*Stuffed elements that overlap from one side of the garment front to the other, and snap or velcro in place

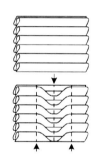

seam insertion of ric rac

Prairie points: Cut a square of cloth. Fold in half, wrong sides together. Fold the left corner down to the bottom center. Fold the right corner down to the bottom center. Prairie points may be used individually, in groups, in graduated sizes, etc.

Metallic Thread: stitch (quilt) a particular area, outline an element on the garment, couch around the edge of a motif, thread through the lace, couch around a motif on lace...

Textured add-ons:
Beads: available in craft shops or fabric shops, either as individual beads, in a tube, in a bag (bridal shops have various shapes), or on a string; take apart a necklace or other jewelry for unusual beads; craft shops sometimes have wooden, glass, pottery, clay, metal beads in interesting shapes (square, rectangular, oval, etc.)

Beads can be used to emphasize a portion of a design (center on flower), or sewn on the dots of the printed fabric, or to form petals on a blossom, or strung on ribbons, etc.

Buttons: New: can include pewter, clay, glass, or home-made (see below); *Old:* rescue off garment: check garage sales, junk shops, etc.

REMEMBER: buttons don't have to be used to close the garment ... they can be stitched on anywhere for added texture, to emphasize a detail (ex: center of a flower, eye on a creature, etc.), sewn in a clump, etc.
    TO MAKE BUTTONS: Using polymer clay (available at art supply stores), mold and shape buttons which can then be baked firm in your oven. (See Sources, page 32)

Additional Texture:
Pleats: segments of cloth can have tucks or pleats (even, uneven, straight, or angled) sewn in before it is sewn into garment:
    IDEA: after pleated segment is sewn in, stitch through the center of the pleated portion, so instead of lying flat, the pleats are twisted to lay in the opposite direction through the center...

Gathers: try doing a grid of running stitch on a piece of cloth, then gathering all threads slightly to form a piece of 'seeksucker'...

Seam insertions: lace, cording (purchased or self-made), piping, prairie points, ric-rac (can be sewn in seam so only half of it sticks out)... ric rac can also be braided, gathered, coiled, etc...

Dangles: ribbons, rat-tail cord, strung shells...

Decorating Ideas:
Include in your patchwork: bits of embroidery (great way to use up projects that were started but never finished...can include counted cross stitch, blackwork, hardanger, crewel embroidery, needlepoint, etc.)

Stencil a design on cloth and include it in your patchwork, or paint certain areas of fabric (sponge or spattered). Remember that you can stencil or paint on printed cloth as well as solid...

Tea-dye fabric for inclusion in your piece. It's a great way to tone down bright fabrics...

Worn doilies, lace, dresser scarves, tablecloths, etc. Use the good segments (possible to use as insertions in seams or as collars or cuffs)

May want to put sleeves on.... try ripping fabric into strips (3/4" wide) and knitting or crocheting sleeves...

Unusual Sources for Add-ons:
Try fishing supply places ... some of the 'spoons' used with hooks are beautiful, and they have a hole through the end, so they can be sewn onto the garment...

Craft Stores: beads, buttons, shells, ribbons...

Bridal Fabric Shops: beads, lace, ribbons, appliqués...

Salvation Army or Second-hand Clothing Stores: for items that can be taken off clothing and reused...

Rummage Sales: doilies, lace, bits of needlework, buttons, jewelry that can be disassembled...

Yarn Shops: source of unusual buttons...

Left to Right:
Linda Halpin: Tunic Length Bog Coat with inset pockets and piping accents
Lynn Shepson: Tunic Length Bog Coat with Seminole Patchwork banding
Amanda Halpin: Tunic Length Bog Coat with piping accents

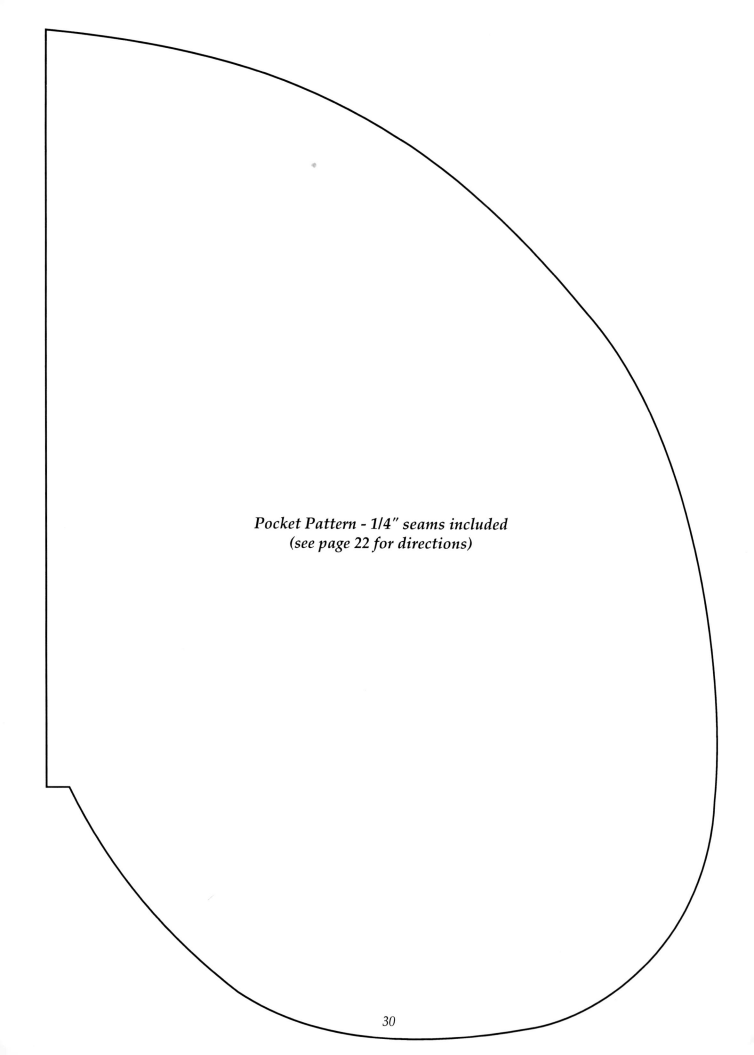

Pocket Pattern - 1/4" seams included
(see page 22 for directions)

Design Sheet for Cutting Requirements:

Use this page to design your next Bog Coat!

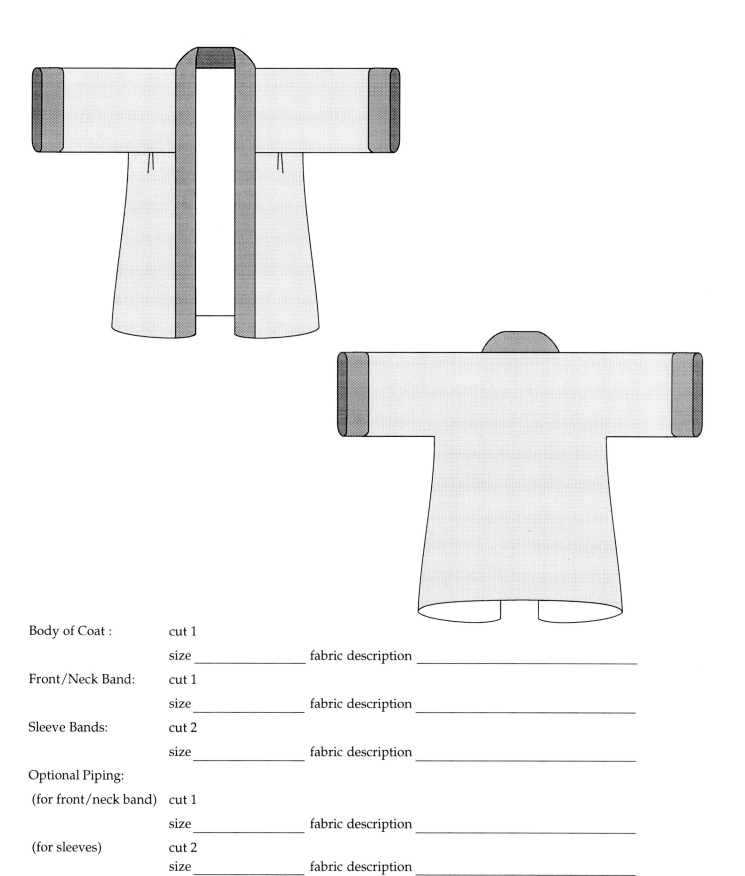

Body of Coat :   cut 1

                             size _____ fabric description _____

Front/Neck Band: cut 1

                             size _____ fabric description _____

Sleeve Bands: cut 2

                             size _____ fabric description _____

Optional Piping:

(for front/neck band)   cut 1

                             size _____ fabric description _____

(for sleeves)   cut 2

                             size_____ fabric description _____

Resources for Quilted Clothing, Embellishments, Techniques

Books:
(Listed by Title)

Appliqué a la Mode (information on appliqué, three-dimensional blossoms)
by Linda Halpin © 1992
RCW Publishing, Columbia Cross Roads, PA 16914

Basic Seminole Patchwork
by Cheryl Greider Bradkin © 1990
Leone Publications, 2628 Bayshore Drive, Mt. View, CA 94043

Curved Strip - Piecing
by Marilyn Stothers © 1988
PH Press, Winnipeg, Manitoba Canada

Cut My Cote (history of clothing styles)
by Dorothy K. Burnham © 1973
Royal Ontario Museum, Toronto

Design and Sew It Yourself: A Workbook for Creative Clothing
by Lois Ericson and Diane Ericson Frode © 1983
available through Lois Ericson, PO Box 5222, Salem, OR 97304

Ethnic Costume: Clothing Design & Techniques with an International Inspiration
by Lois Ericson & Diane Ericson © 1979
Van Nostrand Reinhold Company, New York, NY

The Great Put On: Sew Something Smashing
by Lois Ericson and Linda Wakefield © 1992
Erics' Press; available through Lois Ericson, PO Box 5222, Salem, OR 97304

Pieced Clothing and **Pieced Clothing Variations**
by Yvonne Porcella © 1980
Porcella Studios, 3619 Shoemake Avenue, Modesto, CA 95351

Putting on the Glitz: Unusual Fabrics & Threads for Quilting & Sewing
by Sandra Hatch and Ann Boyce © 1991
Chilton Book Company, Radnor, PA

Quilted Clothing
by Jean Ray Laury © 1982
Oxmoor House, P.O. Box 2463, Birmingham, AL 35201

The New Clay (beads, buttons, jewelry, etc. out of polymer clay)
by Nan Roche © 1991
Flower Valley Press, Rockville, MD; available through Aardvark Adventures

Wearable Art For Real People
by Mary Mashuta © 1989
C & T Publishing, 5021 Blum Road, #1, Martinez, CA 94553

Wonderful Wearables: A Celebration of Creative Clothing
by Virginia Avery © 1991
American Quilter's Society, P.O. Box 3290, Paducah, KY 42002-3290

Notions:

Aardvark Adventures
P.O. Box 2449, Livermore, CA 94551-2449
Catalog $1: beads, variety of fibers, unusual findings, polymer clay

Clotilde, Inc.
1909 SW First Ave. Ft. Lauderdale, FL 33315
Catalog $1: threads, books, videos, notions, Ultrasuede scraps

Hand-Dyed Fabrics: New York Beauty Dye Works by Sheryll Robbins
604 N. Madison Street, Rome, NY 13440

Books by Linda Halpin:
Patches of Time © **1991**
Appliqué a la Mode © **1992**
Beyond the Bog Coat © **1993**
available at fine quilting stores